We're Going to the Mountains

Written by Steve Kemp • Illustrated by Lisa Horstman

2008 Great Smoky Mountains Association

We're going to the mountains

Oh the sights we shall *see*

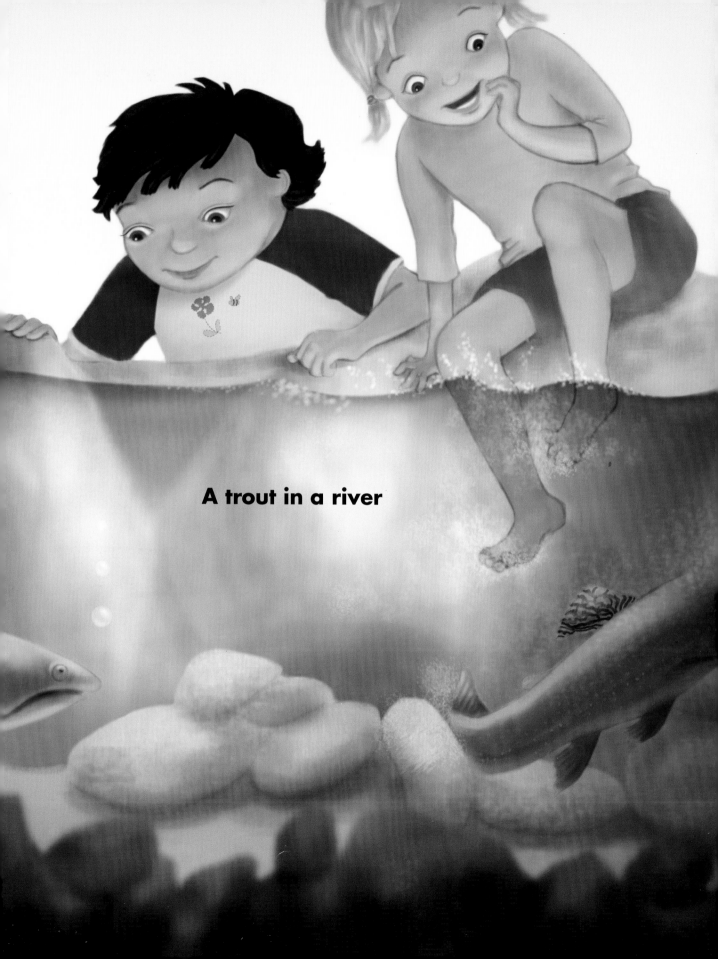

A trout in a river

A bear in a tree.

We're going to the mountains
Oh the sounds we shall *hear*

The song of a sparrow

The snort of a deer.

We're going to the mountains
Oh the smells we shall *smell*

A white spotted skunk

A fragrant bluebell.

We're going to the mountains
Oh the trails we shall *walk*

Through forests so quiet
We won't want to talk.

We're going to the mountains
Oh the roads we shall *ride*

So steep and so curvy
Our eyes open wide.

We're going to the mountains
Oh the streams we shall *follow*

We're Going to the Mountains

by Steve Kemp • illustrations by Lisa Horstman

From Grandma & Grandpa Gentry
August 2014 - Upon return from
the Smoky Mountains.

We hope you can go to the mountains
with us some time.

We love you!

© 2008 Great Smoky Mountains Association
Edited by Steve Kemp & Kent Cave
Designed by Lisa Horstman
Printed in Canada

5 6 7 8 9

ISBN 978-0-937207-59-8

Great Smoky Mountains Association is a nonprofit organization which supports the educational, scientific, and historical programs of Great Smoky Mountains National Park. Our publications are an educational service intended to enhance the public's understanding and enjoyment of the national park. If you would like to know more about our publications, memberships, and projects, please contact:

Great Smoky Mountains Association
P.O. Box 130
Gatlinburg, TN 37738 • 865-436-7318
www.SmokiesInformation.org

For my lovely niece and stinky nephews, because we always have a blast when they come to the mountains. —Steve Kemp

For all of the brave parents who grit their teeth and drag their kids away from their cell phones for a few hours to see the mountains. And for Dave. —Lisa Horstman

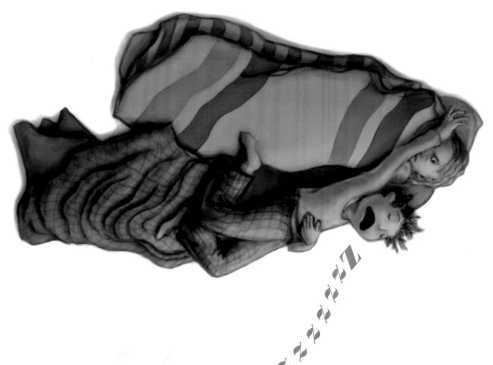

When the stars shine so bright
They don't even seem real.

We're going to the mountains
Oh the sleep we shall **sleep**

Under thick woolen blankets piled ten inches deep.

Where cold waters tumble
From highland to hollow.

We're going to the mountains
Oh the thoughts we shall *think*

Like where does a snake go
When a snake needs a drink?

We're going to the mountains
Oh the peace we shall *feel*